XTREME RACES
INDIANAPOLIS 500

BY S.L. HAMILTON

Visit us at
www.abdopublishing.com

Published by ABDO Publishing Company, PO Box 398166, Minneapolis, MN 55439.
Copyright ©2013 by Abdo Consulting Group, Inc. International copyrights reserved in all countries. No part of this book may be reproduced in any form without written permission from the publisher. A&D Xtreme™ is a trademark and logo of ABDO Publishing Company.

Printed in the United States of America, North Mankato, Minnesota.
102012
012013

 PRINTED ON RECYCLED PAPER

Editor: John Hamilton
Graphic Design: Sue Hamilton
Cover Design: John Hamilton
Cover Photo: Getty Images
Interior Photos: All photos AP except: Alamy-pgs 6-7; Corbis-pgs 4-5 & 21 (Janet Guthrie photo); Getty Images-pgs 1, 8-9, & 21 (Johnny Rutherford & Bobby Unser photos); ThinkStock-flag graphic.

ABDO Booklinks
Web sites about Great Races are featured on our Book Links pages. These links are routinely monitored and updated to provide the most current information available.
Web site: www.abdopublishing.com

Cataloging-in-Publication Data

Hamilton, Sue L., 1959-
 Indianapolis 500 / S.L. Hamilton.
   p. cm. -- (Xtreme races)
Includes index.
ISBN 978-1-61783-694-7
1. Indianapolis Speedway Race--History--Juvenile literature. 2. Indianapolis Speedway Race--Juvenile literature. 3. Automobile racing--Indiana--Speedway--Juvenile literature. 4. Indy cars--Juvenile literature.   I. Title.
796.7206--dc23
                          2012945884

Racers take a warm-up lap during the 2012 running of the Indianapolis 500 at the Indianapolis Motor Speedway in Speedway, Indiana. Speedway is a town within the city limits of Indianapolis.

History of the Race

In 1911, automobile businessman Carl Fisher of Indianapolis, Indiana, wanted one long race that would draw a huge crowd that would stay for the day. Fisher and his partners came up with the "International 500-Mile Sweepstakes Race."

XTREME FACT – In 1911, the loose rock on the Indianapolis Motor Speedway's racetrack was replaced with 3.2 million bricks to make it safer. This led to the track's nickname: "The Brickyard."

Ray Harroun wins the first Indy 500 in his Marmon Wasp.

On May 30, 1911, more than 80,000 people paid $1 to watch the 500-mile (805 km) event. Winner Ray Harroun won in 6 hours, 42 minutes, and 8 seconds. The race became known as the Indianapolis 500.

The first Indianapolis 500 at the Indianapolis Motor Speedway on May 30, 1911.

THE TRACK

The Indianapolis 500 takes place at the Indianapolis Motor Speedway (IMS) in Speedway, Indiana. The 2.5-mile (4-km) oval track has four turns and straightaways. This is the original layout created when the track first opened in 1909.

Once surfaced in bricks, the IMS track was paved over with asphalt in sections beginning in 1936. Today, only the 3-foot (.9-m) start/finish line shows the original bricks. This is called the "Yard of Bricks."

XTREME FACT – The IMS is the world's largest spectator sporting facility, with more than 250,000 seats. Churchill Downs, Yankee Stadium, the Rose Bowl, the Roman Colosseum and Vatican City can all fit inside the IMS oval, which covers 253 acres (102 ha). There is even part of a golf course inside the oval!

THE RULES

Thirty-three cars compete in an Indy 500 race. They have very specific requirements. All have the same chassis. Teams choose engines from one of three manufacturers: Chevrolet, Honda, or Lotus. By having similar vehicles, the ability to win depends more on driver skill.

XTREME FACT – A 200-page rulebook spells out the specific rules for the racers.

11

How to Qualify

To compete in the Indianapolis 500, drivers race in time trials to see who is the fastest. Drivers are given three chances to qualify. The fastest drivers start the race at the front of the pack.

XTREME FACT – *The "pole position" is the inside front row. It is considered the best spot to start. It goes to the driver with the best time after all drivers have had a chance to qualify.*

The fastest qualifiers for the 2012 Indianapolis 500 were Ryan Hunter-Reay (left), James Hinchcliffe (center), and Ryan Briscoe (right) in the pole position.

THE START

The Indy 500 begins with 11 rows of 3 cars. They follow a pace car around the track to warm up their tires. When the pace car moves off the track, racers get the green flag. The announcer says, "Indianapolis 500 is green!" The cars speed up to more than 225 mph (362 kph). As they cross the starting line, the 33 cars are separated by mere feet. Hearts race and palms sweat. Each driver wants to make history.

XTREME QUOTE – *"It is the most intense, frightening mixture of fumes and cars and tires and walls and people and personalities."*
—Driver Eddie Cheever describing the start of the Indy 500

26
27
28
29
30
31
32
33

STRATEGY TO WIN

Weather conditions and driver skill often determine the winner of the Indy 500. If the weather is hot, tires will begin to melt and make the track slippery. Drivers must slow down on the turns.

Ryan Briscoe leads the pack on a turn on a hot race day at the 2012 Indianapolis 500.

Quick pit stops save precious seconds. Drafting involves driving directly behind another vehicle. It saves fuel and allows drivers to slingshot past the competition. The Indy 500 is a long race. Drivers must stay focused and alert.

XTREME QUOTE – "It's a long race and the fastest car doesn't necessarily win."
—Driver Scott Dixon, 2008 Indianapolis 500 winner

DANGERS

High speeds, lightweight cars, slick tracks, and concrete walls combine to make the Indianapolis 500 a very dangerous race. From 1911-2012, 35 drivers have died at the event. Safety measures help, but lives are still at risk.

Driver Mike Conway goes airborne on the last lap of the 2010 Indy 500. Conway collided with an out-of-gas car and was propelled into the catch fence. Conway survived with leg and back injuries. The newest chassis for Indy cars is designed to help prevent cars from going airborne.

FAMOUS DRIVERS

The Indianapolis 500 usually takes more than thre
hours to complete. Only top drivers become multip
winners of The Greatest Spectacle in Racing.

*Three drivers have won the Indy 500 four times: A.J. Foy
Al Unser, and Rick Mears.*

A.J. Foyt won in 1961, 1964, 1967, and 1977.

Al Unser won in 1970, 1971, 1978, and 1987.

Rick Mears won in 1979, 1984, 1988, and 1991.

A.J. Foyt was the first 4-time Indy 500 winner. He raced a record 35 consecutive times from 1958 to 1992. He earned the pole position 4 times.

Al Unser's four Indy 500 wins were made over the course of 17 years. His 1970 and 1971 victories make him one of only five drivers to have back-to-back wins.

Rick Mears became a four-time Indy 500 winner after only 14 starts, the least of any 4-time winner. He earned the pole position 6 times, the record as of 2012.

Seven drivers have won the Indy 500 three times.

Louis Meyer won in 1928, 1933, and 1936.

Wilbur Shaw won in 1937, 1939, and 1940.

Mauri Rose won in 1941, 1947, and 1948.

Johnny Rutherford won in 1974, 1976, and 1980.

Bobby Unser won in 1968, 1975, and 1981.

Hélio Castroneves won in 2001, 2002, and 2009.

Dario Franchitti won in 2007, 2010, and 2012.

Three generations of Unsers. Al Unser Jr. (left), Al Unser III (center), Al Unser Sr (right).

The Unsers are the most winning family at the Indy 500. Al Unser won 4 times. Bobby (Al's older brother) won 3 times. Al Jr. (Al's son) won 2 times. Other Unser family members have also raced: Jerry Unser (Al and Bobby's older brother), his son Johnny, and Bobby's son Robby.

Janet Guthrie raced in 4 Indy 500s from 1977-80.

Danica Patrick raced in 7 Indy 500s from 2005-11.

Janet Guthrie was the first woman to drive in the Indianapolis 500 in 1977. Car problems forced her to quit. In 1978, she finished in 9th place. As of 2012, only 11 women have raced in the Indy 500. Danica Patrick was the highest finisher. She placed 3rd in 2009.

FAMOUS CARS

After more than 100 years of racing, there have been dramatic changes in Indy cars. The 1911 Marmon Wasp (front row right, #32) had an average speed of 75 mph (120 kph). Ray Harroun won the race in 6 hours, 42 minutes, 8 seconds.

Thirty-three winning Indy 500 cars sit on the track to celebrate the Indianapolis Motor Speedway's 100th anniversary in 2010.

1961 Bowes Seal Fast Bignotti

2010 Target Chip Ganassi Racing Car

A.J. Foyt's 1961 Bowes Seal Fast Bignotti (front row left, #1) had an average speed of 139 mph (224 kph). Foyt won his first Indy 500 in 3 hours, 35 minutes, 37 seconds. Dario Franchitti's 2010 Target Chip Ganassi Racing Car (front row center, #10) sped around the track at an average speed of 162 mph (260 kph). Franchitti won in 3 hours, 5 minutes and 37 seconds.

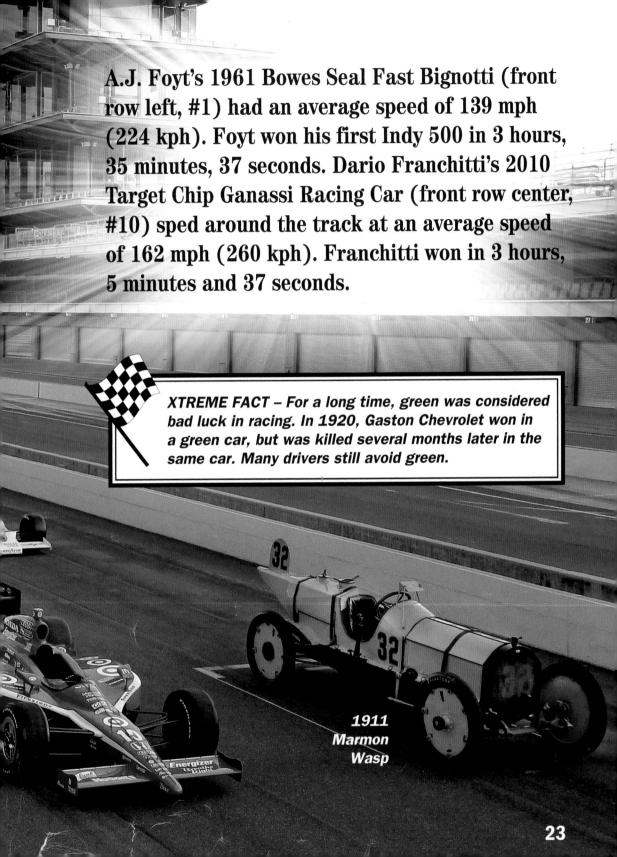

XTREME FACT – For a long time, green was considered bad luck in racing. In 1920, Gaston Chevrolet won in a green car, but was killed several months later in the same car. Many drivers still avoid green.

1911 Marmon Wasp

INDY TRADITIONS

One of the most famous Indy 500 traditions is for the winner to drink milk. It began in 1933. Winner Louis Meyer asked for a glass of buttermilk. A dairy company thought this would be a great way to advertise. In 1936, Meyer won again. A bottle of milk was waiting for him. The milk tradition stopped briefly from 1947-1955. But since 1956, all Indy 500 winners have celebrated with an ice-cold bottle of milk.

Winner Hélio Castroneves celebrates in 2009.

XTREME FACT – Indy 500 winners can choose between whole, two percent, or skim milk to celebrate their victory.

Driver Dan Wheldon kisses the "Yard of Bricks" after winning the 2005 Indianapolis 500. Wheldon also won the 2011 Indy 500. Tragically, he was killed in a racing accident in October 2011.

Indy 500 winners today give the Indianapolis Motor Speedway's start/finish line a grateful kiss. This is called "kissing the bricks." Another tradition is the Winner's Wreath. Driver Jim Rathmann was the first to receive a wreath of flowers for his 1960 win. Today, the wreath is made of 33 orchids mixed with 33 small checkered flags. They represent the 33 cars that start the race.

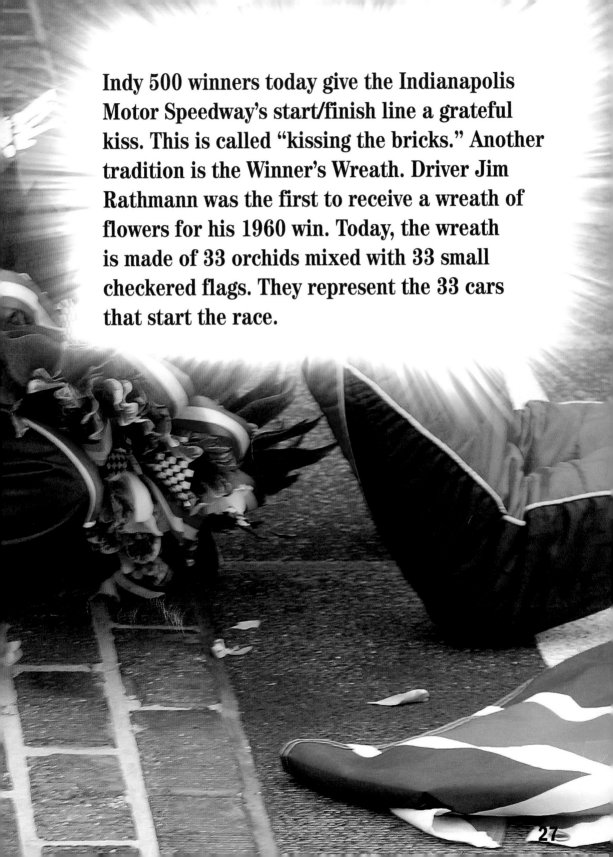

THE FINISH

After 500 miles (804 km), a winner crosses the brick-covered finish line with a wave of the checkered flag. Since 1936, winners have been awarded the Borg-Warner Trophy. More than 5 feet (1.5 m) tall, the trophy features each winner. It is one of the most desired trophies in auto racing.

The 2012 Indianapolis 500 champion Dario Franchitti poses next to the Borg-Warner Trophy.

GLOSSARY

BORG-WARNER TROPHY
The trophy awarded to the winners of the Indianapolis 500. The trophy is made of sterling silver and weighs about 110 pounds (50 kg). It was originally created in 1935 by the Borg-Warner Automotive Company at a cost of $10,000.

CATCH FENCE
The tall fence that surrounds a racetrack. The fence is designed to catch out-of-control race cars, as well as protect fans from cars, broken metal, loose tires, etc.

CHASSIS
The body or frame of a vehicle. The chassis on Indianapolis 500 race cars are identical.

DRAFTING
When race cars are purposely driven one behind another. The distance between cars is extremely close. Mere inches may separate them. This bold driving technique is called drafting, or slipstreaming. The vehicle in back burns less gas and has an easier time driving through the air. At the appropriate time, the back vehicle's driver will slingshot out from behind the other car, moving at a faster speed and likely passing the front car.

INDY CAR
A type of single-seat, open cockpit, open-wheel racing car found at such races as the Indianapolis 500.

PIT STOP
During a race, a stop just off the track where the race car is serviced by the pit crew with such things as refueling, tire changes, and mechanical checks. This is done as quickly as possible. The speed at which a pit crew completes the vehicle's servicing can make or break a race.

POLE POSITION
In a race, the inside front row position. It is generally thought that the pole position is the best place to start. In the Indianapolis 500, the driver with the fastest qualifying time is given the pole position.

YARD OF BRICKS
The Indianapolis Motor Speedway's 3-foot (or one yard) (.9 m) start/finish line that is paved with the original bricks that once covered all of the track. Beginning in 1936, asphalt was used to pave over rougher parts where the bricks had broken. By October 1961, all of the bricks had been paved over with asphalt except for the "Yard of Bricks."

INDEX